The Rosary

a way into prayer

ANNE VAIL

Wood engravings by David Jones

CANTERBURY
PRESS
Norwich

Text © Anne Vail 1997
Illustrations © David Jones 1924
First published 1997 by The Canterbury Press Norwich
(a publishing imprint of Hymns Ancient & Modern Limited,
a registered charity)
St Mary's Works, St Mary's Plain,
Norwich, Norfolk, NR3 3BH

Bible quotations are taken from the
Douay-Rheims version published in 1899

British Library Cataloguing in Publication Data

A catalogue record for this book is available
from the British Library

ISBN 1–85311–160–0

*Typeset by David Gregson Associates, Beccles, Suffolk and
Printed and bound in Great Britain by
St Edmundsbury Press Limited, Bury St Edmunds, Suffolk*

*The author would like to express her gratitude to the Trustees of
the David Jones Estate for their kind permission to reprint these timeless
wood engravings.*

Contents

David Jones

David Jones was born in Kent in 1885. His talent has been described as the greatest dual talent since Blake, for David Jones' war poetry is amongst the finest written, and he is recognised as one of the most gifted and sensitive British watercolour painters of the 20th century.

He returned from the First World War profoundly influenced by his experiences and was received into the Catholic Church in 1923. The following year he joined the sculptor and engraver Eric Gill, founder of the Guild of St Joseph and St Dominic at Ditchling in Sussex, with whom he shared an interest in the beauty of early Christian art.

With the freedom of his new found faith, David Jones embarked on a series of wood engravings of religious subjects. In 1924 the Child's Rosary Book was privately printed at Ditchling, from which the wood engravings in this book are reproduced. They are a glowing example of his new conception of the nature of art. Not only as a Catholic, but as an artist, David Jones recognised and drew strength from the doctrine of the inseparability of spirit and matter, which is so particularly apt in the undertaking of the illustration of the mysteries of the rosary.

In these works the figures of the saints, and of Our Lady in particular, are engraved with tenderness and sympathy, the soldiers are reminiscent of those with whom he shared trench and billet on the Western Front, and the animals are drawn with almost Franciscan affection. These linear designs are the forerunner of his mature work, with its highly imaginative view of the world suffused with spirituality. David Jones died in 1974 and since then there has been a growing awareness of his extraordinary talent.

Part One: The Beads

The Circlet of Beads

The name 'rosary' is given to the small circlet of beads which is so familiar to its devotees as to be taken for granted, although to some people it is a rather strange relic of a bygone age. The very simplicity of most rosaries, crammed into laden pockets, gives them a matter-of-fact image, rather like a keyring or a fountain pen. They are part of the 'luggage' of many Christians, and even those who may have only a muddled idea of the prayer of the rosary still carry their beads, as if the small circlet provides some sort of spiritual insurance.

The word 'bede' originally meant 'prayer', and to 'bid one's bedes' was a literal reference to saying one's prayers. In the sixteenth century the word 'bede' or 'bead' was freed from its religious association but by then the word 'rosary' had come to refer to the circlet of beads with which we are familiar.

But why do we need to count our prayers anyway? It is hard to find any area of human activity which we do not seek to quantify. Some of us seem to be almost obsessed with numbers and seem curiously satisfied with any statement that is backed up by a statistic. Prayer can be the most elusive and frustrating activity as well as the most sublime experience and there is no reason why it, too, should not be subject to our desire for order and regulation. Sometimes we need to count our prayers in order to know how many we have said and where we are in the sequence of the prayer we are saying.

Ways of counting prayer were very important to Christians of the eleventh century, many of whom participated in the daily monastic prayer which included the recitation and chanting of the 150 psalms. The abbeys were the centres of learning and few people beyond the walls of monasteries were able to read or write. Those who came in from the villages and fields to join the monks at prayer might have been reduced to being little more than onlookers if someone had not had the bright idea of tying 150 knots in a length of string. With the help of this practical device the lay people were able to recite the Pater Noster (Our Father) in response to each of the 150 Psalms. The origin of our expression 'pitter patter' is said to come from the sound of their whispered prayer.

On their return from Jerusalem and the east, the medieval crusaders brought glowing accounts of prayer beads they had seen in use amongst the Muslims and their reports influenced the development of different types of prayer beads in Europe. The custom of counting prayers on beads had therefore been in existence long before the rosary became popular in the fourteenth century.

In 1041 William of Malmesbury presents us with evidence of the first recorded use of beads for prayer, apart from the counting of Pater Nosters. He describes the beads of Lady Godiva as a circlet of threaded jewels on which she was wont to number her prayers in honour of the Blessed Virgin and which she bequeathed to be hung around the neck of the statue of Mary in the church at Coventry where she lived.

In fourteenth-century England prayer beads were given the name 'rosary' for the rose was not only the symbol of Our Lady but of England itself. Devotion to Mary had become part of English culture and England had come to be known as Our Lady's Dowry. Although this title fell into comparative disuse it has never been relinquished – and the rose remains the symbol of England.

Until the Reformation in the sixteenth century, roses

were woven into chaplets or crowns which would be placed on statues of Mary on her feast days. The connection was strengthened by biblical allusion: 'I am the rose of Sharon' (Song of Songs 2:1) and, 'Like a rose planted on the rivers I have budded forth (Ecclesia sticus 24:14). Rose gardens became an accepted image of paradise and in monastic gardens 'the paradise' was cultivated by the monks.

As prayer beads became popular, the rich spent vast sums on threaded jewels, and the courts of Europe positively sparkled with the rosaries of the nobility.

Today, we are increasingly aware of the finite nature of the world's resources and are able to treasure natural materials. The quality of wood or of glass can be almost as precious to us as the jewels of a previous age. Modern prayer beads are generally more sober and discreet than in earlier days and echo the knots of string used by medieval Christians – we seem to have come full circle and rediscovered that the basic role of prayer beads is to help us to count our prayers. They are of course of secondary importance to the prayer itself.

Our Lady's Psalter

The prayer of the rosary evolved in the thirteenth century from the teaching of St Dominic, who travelled from Castille in Spain to the Languedoc in the South of France in 1206. There, Dominic and his companions spent several years preaching to people suffering the indoctrination of a heretical sect known as the Albigensians, after the town of Albi where they had established themselves. Albigensianism was an updated version of a far older heresy known as Manicheeism, a creed of despair.

All that was material and human was vilified in their teaching. Instead of seeing life and the human body as gifts of a loving God, and the world in which he placed man as a source of beauty and the means of sustaining life, everything bodily and material was viewed as an evil from which man should turn with loathing. The real meaning of life was lost and the resulting desolation frequently led to suicide. Because the Albigensians utterly rejected the New Testament narrative of Christ's life, and their doctrine was based on the perpetual conflict between spirit and flesh, St Dominic spoke to them of the Incarnation and of the great love of God who sent his only Son into the world to die for our sins in order that we might be reunited with him.

His teaching was based on biblical wisdom infused with love and it was an immense task that could only be accomplished by Dominic's profound spirituality so that his listeners were touched not only by the elaborate logic he uttered, but above all by the power of prayer.

Since all that was part of bodily experience was held to be evil, what more effective means could there be than the unceasing contemplation of Christian virtues in the lives of the holy family. The prayers Dominic recited to accompany this were the Our Father – the prayer that Jesus taught us, the Hail Mary – the oldest and simplest of Christian salutations, and the Gloria, acknowledging that all honour is due to him who created the universe. By reciting these most familiar of prayers the mind was able, without wandering, to hold on to the truth of the scene and to understand its meaning.

Before the name 'rosary' came into general use, this form of prayer was widely known as 'Our Lady's Psalter' because the 150 Hail Marys to be recited reflected the 150 Psalms in the Bible.

By its division into fifteen parts, each commemorating an event in the life of our Lord and the Blessed Virgin, St Dominic sought to impress the Scripture narrative more deeply into the minds and hearts of his people so that each scene became more vivid and palpably real.

We know therefore that the prayer of the rosary evolved into the form we know today during the thirteenth century, a time when devotion to the Blessed Virgin had a practical, earthy approach. The words of the Song of Songs, 'an enclosed garden, a fountain sealed up', were taken to heart for they symbolized the womb that bore the Redeemer. And to St Dominic who, according to his thirteenth-century chronicler Bernard Gui 'glowed with fervour of his devotion to the Virgin Mother of God', the true answer to the Albigensians was to be found in the image of the holy family and the miracle of the Incarnation.

Nowadays the rosary is generally divided into three groups of fifty Hail Marys – the Joyful Mysteries, the Sorrowful Mysteries and the Glorious Mysteries.

Many people find it hard to accept the repetitive nature of the prayer of the rosary, but repeated rhythm is an essential part of our lives. Indeed our entire being and existence is subject to repetition. All that surrounds us moves in unceasing rhythm, as the sun rises and sets, the seasons follow each other and growth is sustained by their sequence. The pulse of life itself is defined by constant movement. There can be something profoundly soothing in the repetition of words when we realize that those same words have been repeated daily for some eight centuries. If the rosary had merely been a prayer of mindless repetition, it would surely have ceased to hold any attraction long ago. The word 'mantra' is sometimes used in connection with the rosary, and since the dictionary defines this as an instrument of thought, there is a compelling reason for the choice.

The rosary has been compared to the image of a child sitting on his mother's lap, fingering the beads of her necklace and murmuring to her while she turns the pages of a book before his eyes. For the prayer is based on meditation on the life of Christ as described in the New Testament, with Mary as our guide.

The first cycle of the rosary contains the Joyful Mysteries, which deal with the events surrounding the serene yet overshadowed youth of Jesus. The Sorrowful Mysteries follow his passion from the garden of Gethsemane to death on the cross. The third cycle, the Glorious Mysteries, portray the Resurrection, the Ascension, the Descent of the Holy Spirit and finally the Assumption of Mary and her Coronation in Heaven.

We enter this quiet and holy world with the help of the Blessed Virgin who witnessed so many of these events: 'His mother kept all these words in her heart' (Luke 2:51). These beautiful words from the Gospel of St Luke give the impression that much of what

9

happened was not readily, or at least immediately, understood even by Mary.

Catechisms have described a mystery as a revealed truth which is beyond our reason. The mention of 'mystery' is something that immediately alerts and intrigues the mind, as any writer or reader of thriller fiction is aware. Although we know in faith that some things are beyond our understanding this does not stop us from exploring the possibilities.

Obviously we will never be able to understand fully the truths of faith because we are finite while God is infinite. But some small reflection of the glory of God can nevertheless be glimpsed, for example in the complexity and beauty of nature. Such 'glimpses' can prompt us to wonder at the mind of the Creator by whom all is sustained although the reality is far beyond our comprehension.

To mystics like St Francis of Assisi, the hand of the Creator was vividly present in his creation, and Francis speaks joyfully of 'brother sun' and 'sister moon'. Perhaps we too can catch a glimpse of his vision through the mysteries of the rosary in which we see not only the truths of our destiny in the grand sense, but on a more mundane level gain a sense of proportion in the midst of the muddle of our lives. Even those events we may count as nothing can assume an immense value as we see the hand of the Holy Spirit moving quietly through all that we do and all that happens to us.

A friend once told me that while meditating on the mysteries of the rosary, in his mind he first placed himself within the scene that was taking place, so that when the angel Gabriel appeared to Mary at the Annunciation, he quietly seated himself in the shadows and watched. The event became more astonishing and moving each time he did this. Imagining himself present at each of the Joyful Mysteries of the rosary he saw the serenity of the life of the holy family, the courage and trust of Our Lady and St Joseph; the patience and loyalty of Simeon and Anna as they waited in the temple, and the fear of Mary and Joseph when they lost their Child, only to find him in the temple surrounded by the elders.

The Sorrowful Mysteries became for him the image of a turbulent world, of cruelty and cowardice. He watched the despair and loneliness of the scene in the garden of Gethsemane, the mindless brutality of the soldiers and the crowd, the compassion shown to the grieving women, the courage of Veronica and Simon of Cyrene, and ultimately the loneliness and desolation of the cross.

Among the images passing before him, one constantly recurred. In sixteenth- and seventeenth-century paintings, Mary has so often been portrayed as a figure weeping and swooning with grief at the foot of the cross. St John says simply that she stood at the foot of the cross and the image of this figure standing unflinching before the dying figure of her Son in humility, prayer and silence, the model for every Christian, is one that filled him with awe.

The Glorious Mysteries can appear as an extraordinary example of human bewilderment in the face of the workings of heaven. We are led through the incredulous visits to the empty tomb, the unspeakable joy of the apostles as the truth finally dawns on them that Jesus has indeed risen and is amongst them once more. At the Descent of the Holy Spirit and the foundation of the Church they are filled with courage and holiness. Finally comes the Coronation of the Blessed Virgin in heaven which is the fulfilment of the promise given to us all, 'I shall return to take you to myself so that you may be with me where I am' (John 14:3). These

11

momentous events find an echo in our everyday lives and cannot leave us untouched. As we meditate on the mysteries of the rosary we recognize familiar faces and percieve events which recur in our lives, albeit in different guises. All this is brought to mind through the gentle repitition of the Hail Mary as we enter a world in which our thoughts move with freedom limited only by the gentle rhythm of prayer.

Catechisms describe prayer as the 'raising up of the mind and heart to God' and the prayer of the rosary is an example of this. We turn our thoughts to the Scriptures and in calling to mind any event from the life of Christ as portrayed in the Gospels we can only become aware of his compassion, his gentleness with repentant sinners, his meekness and his humility. As these become increasingly evident we can hardly remain indifferent.

A Prayer for all Occasions

It is virtually impossible to dwell on the Gospel accounts for any length of time without being swept up into their truth and for one's heart to remain untouched. This is not merely the stuff of dramatic revelation but a means of inspiring one to live by this extraordinary teaching which holds out the promise of the peace for which we long.

But so often our prayer is a garbled plea, snatched at in moments of distress or need, knowing that God understands the turmoil of our lives. And yet we know that we need periods of silence; we need to stop for our spirits to draw breath. And perversely this is something that we put off, almost as if we fear that having once achieved calm, we will not know what to do next. The mere effort of relaxing causes the greatest stress of all.

The world is full of ingenious recipes for meditation and new forms of recreation. And yet the true meaning of the word is 're-creation', the created turning to its Creator. What could be more natural, more vital and to be honest, more daunting? It is all too easy to misconstrue this glaring need of the soul and to become discouraged.

We are obsessed with the care of our physical bodies, and the need for diet and exercise has become almost a religion in itself. The mere suggestion of the damaging effect of pollution on our food can send us into a spiral of panic. And yet the needs of the spirit remain overlooked and we are ill-prepared even to undertake the task of discerning those needs. We feel that it should happen naturally and when it fails to do so, we are disheartened. Subconsciously, we seem to realize the importance of prayer but fail to understand that it is a fundamental part of life. It is as if we are in awe of some august acquaintance, whom we treat with circumspection and shyness, until we come to know that person and, through knowledge, begin to love them and eventually cannot imagine life without them. Ignorance turns many of us away from prayer and the deepest ignorance lies in our misunderstanding of prayer itself. We can sometimes imagine that by means of immense effort and concentration we can achieve great things and this very misconception dooms us to disappointment and failure.

St Paul teaches that we are the temple of the Holy Spirit (1 Corinthians 3:16–17), that he exists within each one of us. We have only to be quiet and listen. We have that wonderful description of the first prayer, 'God walking with Adam and Eve in the cool of the evening' (Genesis 3:8), and it conjures up the intimacy of friend talking to friend.

When we are with a friend and cannot find the right words we have only to be silent and in the silence we can listen. The character of the prayer of the rosary was defined by St Dominic's own form of prayer which consisted of long periods of contemplative silence interrupted only by moments of speech, almost as if he were involved in deep conversation with his Lord. Sometimes his monks would see him thus in rapt attention, on occasion with his head to one side as if listening intently to someone who was addressing words of profound importance to him.

In quiet prayer we frequently find that an echo of our anxieties disturbs and distracts us, rather as one suddenly hears the tick of a clock which has been unnoticed in the general noise, but becomes insistent when silence descends. The world around us is one huge distraction, we are buffeted from one anxiety to another, and it is strange to find in the Middle East that many people are seen to be fingering what look like rosaries but are in fact called worry beads. In time we learn to ignore interruption to our prayer, but there is no doubt that meditative prayer requires practice.

The rosary is of immense value to the learned and unlearned alike, for it can be a great intellectual exercise to those who wish to reflect on the heights of human behaviour, and the ultimate wisdom and mercy of an omnipotent God – an exercise that has taken the lifetime of many saints. At the same time it is a means of immense and simple comfort, but in either case it is a source of great spiritual strength.

It may seem at first that in order to say the rosary at all one needs the skill of a juggler to finger the beads, recite the prayers and meditate. And yet there are many far more complicated sequences that we perform. Driving a car involves steering, changing gear, remaining attentive to the road ahead and keeping a wary eye on the other traffic. Yet we are quite capable of chatting to a companion in the passenger seat.

The rosary is especially the prayer for young parents beset by anxiety and exhaustion and aware of every danger awaiting their children as they grow up in a world alien to innocence. This prayer is infinitely flexible, a decade may be said at any time of day, waiting in a queue or in the silence of the night beside a sleepless child. The compassionate figure of Mary overwhelms us with her solicitude and love, and protects us while for our sakes she exhorts the compassion of her son.

The Heart of the Rosary

The figure of Mary has long been honoured as mother in the churches of east and west, and in the east her title of 'Godbearer' (*Theotokos*) differs only slightly from 'Mother of God' which is more familiar in the west. The remote, almond-eyed yet serene figures of Orthodox iconography, the ornate masterpieces of the Renaissance and the mysterious black madonnas of the South of France all testify to our fascination with Mary as mother of God and of mankind. Yet the inspiration we receive from such human interpretations of Mary is obviously dependent upon the hand of the artist.

We have woven endless legends and wonders around the person of Mary because the ordinary Christian needs to find a means of expressing the weightier judgments of theologians. Some images, statues and mementoes give rise to disapproval but are nevertheless the reminder of a beloved ideal. Who has not gazed on the picture of a loved friend with wistful longing, while remaining perfectly well aware that it is not the picture one loves, but the reality it represents? The value of the picture lies in its ability to focus our attention and to make it easier to bring to mind the face of the living person. For this reason so many of our churches are filled with a happy muddle of statues and pictures. In the same way that we fill our homes with pictures of those whom we love, so we feel as we step from the busy pavement into the quiet of a church that we are entering into the company of the saints. The mind is instantly focused.

In the Middle Ages when most people were unable to read, visual explanations were used in order to clarify theological teaching. Numerous pictures related different aspects of the life of Our Lord in complex detail and many again explained the different roles of the Virgin. In one of these pictures, known as the 'Mantle of Grace', Mary is standing with her arms outstretched over an anxious multitude huddling beneath her star-strewn cape. She pleads on their behalf, reminding her Son that he received his own humanity from her. It is a wonderfully practical explanation of the role of Mary as intercessor, and, at the same time, a vivid portrayal of complex theology. To many this picture demonstrates the reality of the Church and at the same time the holiness that can encompass the vulnerability of mankind. The words 'Hail full of grace' sum up the attitude of the Christian Church to Mary. Despite the brief, almost allusive mention made in the Scriptures of the Blessed Virgin, she has been the sign of Christian mercy and humanity from the earliest times.

In the catacombs, Mary is portrayed as the young mother, symbol of the young Church: the praying heart in whom the identity of the Church is realized. For the Church finds its beginning in the faith of Our Lady at the Annunciation, and as she bears the holy child so she bears the mystery of salvation within her.

In his poem *The Blessed Virgin compared to the air we breathe* Gerard Manley Hopkins has described the mystery of the Incarnation:

> So God was God of old
> A mother came to mould
> Those limbs like ours which are
> What must make our daystar
> Much dearer to mankind
> Whose glory would blind
> Or less would win man's mind
> Through her we may see him

Made sweeter, not made dim
And her hand leaves his light
Sifted to suit our sight

This is the heart of the rosary. The sequence of meditations slowly unravels this deepest of mysteries which
communicates salvation. By dwelling on each mystery
we are drawn into a vision of divine love, in the company of Our Lady as she represents the intended union
of humanity with God, for in her sinless state she is the
perfection of God's creation.

The experience of centuries endorses our allegiance
to Mary as she holds out a vision of peace and reassurance, of hope and trust in the eternal values and ultimately of life over death. She shows us that she is the
perfect example of human obedience, courage and faith
and we feel gratitude towards her which deepens into
affection when the inspiring cause of that gratitude is
understood, as is the reverence we show to her. In the
eighth and ninth centuries, Mary was seen as chosen
by God, pure and chaste, the mediator of the whole
world when in danger, and especially at the hour of
one's death. For who can remain calm in the face of
such uncertainty?

Despite of the solemnity of the subject, there are pictures from earlier days which relate with a light and
almost humorous touch, precisely how Our Lady was
prepared to deal with such a situation. One such picture
known as the 'Scales of Justice' depicts St Michael, the
heavenly judge, standing in all his awesome majesty,
gazing into infinity, unaware of a poor soul, recently
dead, looking anxiously up at him. In his hand
St Michael holds aloft the scales of justice, on one side
the scale of good which looks ominously empty, and on
the other the scale of sins, which not only appears well
filled but, to the horror of the poor soul, its weight is

increased by a series of little devils pulling it further down. In the background, unseen by the anxious soul, stands the figure of the Blessed Virgin dropping her rosary beads one by one into the scale of good, so that to the undisguised amazement of the poor soul, his good deeds satisfactorily come to outweigh his wrong doings. It is not merely a case of wishful thinking, for much theology is portrayed in this picture.

In this century Pope John-Paul has consecrated the whole world to the protection of Mary.

The Rosary – Yesterday and Today

Inspiring examples of the devotion of the people of England and Scotland to the Blessed Virgin Mary and the prayer of the rosary appear in accounts of those who died on the scaffold for their faith at the time of the penal laws during the sixteenth and seventeenth centuries when recitation of the rosary could invite imprisonment, torture and even death.

One Baron Idus of Eckelsdorff was on his travels in Scotland in 1615 and while in Glasgow he came upon the execution of John Ogilvie. The scene might have been of merely passing interest for the Baron held no particular religious views at the time. As the condemned man bade farewell to his friends from the scaffold, he tossed his rosary beads into the crowd, and to Eckelsdorff's surprise they fell into his hands.

He was immediately surrounded by a clamouring crowd, and in an attempt to free himself he quickly relinquished the beads and left the scene. For many years the memory haunted him, and eventually he turned to the Church and was converted. He then thought longingly of John Ogilvie's rosary: 'If I could now get possession of it, I would spare no cost and I would keep it in gold when I got it.' But the opportunity never presented itself again.

For many people today their rosary beads are among their most precious possessions. In times of grave illness the beads are frequently held in acknowledgement of the forgiveness of Christ and the compassion of Our Lady.

One of the effects of the fragmentation of the Christian Church in the sixteenth century was the loss of importance given to Our Lady, to the detriment of much that is gentle and compassionate in the Christian message. The results of such diminishment are far reaching, for experience shows that when devotion to the Blessed Virgin is overlooked, there is frequently a misunderstanding of the Incarnation. One of the many resulting tragedies is the loss of that almost 'domestic' holiness which Mary inspires in family life. Her presence in the family as the mother of God emphasizes that the family is the Church in miniature.

Without this recognition, men and women are in danger of relinquishing the vision of holiness which can be theirs in a truly Christian marriage; the role of motherhood loses its ideal and the sanctity of life itself may be questioned. For this reason, the rosary is the special prayer of the family. The late Father Peyton's expression, 'the family that prays together stays together', is frequently used as evidence of the immense blessing to be gained from family prayer.

The vigilance of Our Lady embraces the whole of humanity. When danger threatens she has frequently appeared in different parts of the world – in France, Portugal, Yugoslavia, South America and numerous other places. Wherever she appears, the message is the same: she calls for penance and prayer and above all for the prayer of the rosary which turns our hearts and souls towards the life, death and resurrection of her Son and ultimately towards peace.

Above all, the prayer of the rosary makes sense of our past, gives value to the present and enables us to face the future with trust in God's love. It is the great prayer of Christian unity and by praying the rosary we are brought nearer to God and through a greater understanding of the mysteries of the scriptures, light is shed on the mystery of our own lives.

Part Two: The Rosary Prayer

Praying the Rosary

Although some religious orders still carry circlets of 150 beads, most rosaries now are made up of five decades, or groups of ten beads, each decade being separated by a larger bead, either square or round, to emphasize the difference.

Attached to the circlet of beads there is a crucifix on a small chain containing three beads. The Apostles' Creed is recited on the crucifix, where we begin, so that at the outset we make an affirmation of our belief.

> *I believe in God, the Father almighty, Creator of hea- ven and earth. And in Jesus Christ, His only Son, our Lord, who was conceived by the Holy Spirit, born of the Virgin Mary, suffered under Pontius Pilate, was crucified, dead and buried; He descended into hell; the third day He rose again from the dead; He ascended into heaven and sitteth on the right hand of God the Father almighty; from thence He shall come to judge the living and the dead. I believe in the Holy Spirit; the holy catholic church; the communion of Saints; the forgiveness of sins; the resurrection of the body and the life everlasting. Amen.*

The creed is followed by three Hail Marys on the three beads above the crucifix. These are offered either for the gifts of faith, hope and charity or sometimes for the grace of devout and uninterrupted prayer.

> *Hail Mary, full of grace, the Lord is with thee: blessed art thou among women, and blessed is the fruit of thy womb, Jesus. Holy Mary, Mother of God, pray for us sinners now and at the hour of our death. Amen.*

Each decade begins with Our Father on the large bead, followed by ten Hail Mary's and ending with the Gloria before beginning the next decade.

> *Our Father who art in heaven, hallowed be Thy name; Thy kingdom come; Thy will be done, on earth as it is in heaven. Give us this day our daily bread and forgive us our trespasses as we forgive those who trespass against us, and lead us not into temptation, but deliver us from evil. Amen.*

> *Glory be to the Father, and to the Son, and to the Holy Spirit. As it was in the beginning, is now, and ever shall be, world without end. Amen.*

There are many ways of reciting the rosary and it is a most practical prayer because it studies the life led by Jesus, precisely because he became man to show us how we should lead our lives.

We may feel that contemplation is the perogative of those in religious life and is too complicated for us. Our thoughts may be confused by tomes of instruction which make us too worried to think about God. But it is really so simple, for to contemplate is to gaze with the mind, in stillness. Some of the Orthodox icons have this stillness about them that prompts the raising of the heart through the mind. The rosary allows for that silence which is essential to prayer.

There is a sense of rhythm in this prayer and in earlier times it was usually recited in procession. And there is no doubt that to recite the rosary when walking, beads in pocket, is a most natural and satisfying way of prayer. The rythmic movement of walking so perfectly matches the pace of the words that it is reminiscent of early piano lessons with a metronome ticking out its sedate rhythm. In the same way, as our hand moves along the beads, our movement itself becomes prayer and without realizing it, we become entirely occupied, mind and body, in praise of God. For some people the rhythmic nature of the prayer suggests song. In France the *Aves* are frequently sung and the melody becomes like a love song, with the theme of the Incarnation and the love of the Blessed Virgin for her Son as the bridge between heaven and earth. For all the mysteries are in reality based on the single theme of the Incarnation.

A friend once told me of her busy London parish where the congregation was so cosmopolitan that the rosary became almost unintelligible with so many different languages, accents and intonations. The problem was solved by each person in turn reciting one decade in his or her own mother tongue. This resulted in a rosary made up of a decade in French, one in Spanish and perhaps one in Swahili. On other occasions the rosary was recited in Latin, for although Latin has ceased to be the language of Catholic worship, it remains a universal language.

Another friend told me that he recited his most rewarding decades while sitting on a crowded bus or tube. As he prayed, his eyes would take in those around him, the lonely and sad, those whose faces were filled with despair, and he would offer his prayer for them.

It is interesting to return to the origins of the rosary to discover that we are not breaking new ground in seeking different ways of reciting the prayer. It has long been the custom to add clauses to the Hail Mary that refer to the theme of the mystery, for example:

Hail Mary, full of grace, the Lord is with thee: blessed art thou amongst women, and blessed is the fruit of thy womb, Jesus – whom you did conceive of the Holy Spirit – Holy Mary, Mother of God, pray for us sinners now and at the hour of our death.

There are many ways in which we can adapt this method without altering the rhythm of our prayer and each person will find his own words. Another example might be taken from the mystery of the crucifixion when we might add, '...and blessed is the fruit of thy womb, Jesus – who is dying on the cross before you – ...' This method can be used in an even more intimate way. We might stop at the words 'Holy Mary, Mother of God, pray for us now' and add, '– when we most need your help – ...' By using this form of prayer we can underline the theme of the mystery either elaborately or quite simply. For example at the nativity mystery, '...blessed is the fruit of thy womb, Jesus – who lies in the manger – ...' or at finding in the temple, '...Holy Mary, Mother of God, pray for us now – that we may also find Jesus – ...' In the Scripture rosary, for example, a short quotation is read from the Scriptures before each Hail Mary, and this becomes a wonderful way of exploring the depth of each mystery. These methods obviously make the prayer much slower. But since the rosary is above all a prayer of meditation, the number of 'extra' meditations may surely vary. We may decide to choose just one decade to dwell upon and expand.

In the eighth and ninth centuries both the Venerable Bede and St Aelred, Abbot of Rievaulx, included the angel's first words, 'Hail, full of grace' in their prayer, for the final 'Holy Mary, Mother of God, pray for us ...' was not added until the fifteenth century. We might follow their example and recite the angelic salutation, and go no further.

Sometimes we may be so preoccupied that we decide to choose an event from the New Testament which has particular significance for our state of mind and to dwell upon it for the entire rosary.

The rhythm of the rosary is maintained in the sequence of days chosen for the different 'mysteries'.

Easter Monday is the Feast of the Angels at the Holy Sepulchre, and Monday is traditionally the day consecrated to the angels. Monday and Thursday are the days of the Joyful Mysteries. Tuesday is the day of the apostles and Friday is the day of the crucifixion. These then are the days of the Sorrowful Mysteries. The Glorious Mysteries are said on Saturday, traditionally the day of Our Lady; Sunday, the holy day of the week; and Wednesday, the day of the Holy Spirit.

However we decide to recite the rosary, the words of Scripture create the 'picture' on which we meditate. In the words of St Benedict, we listen 'with the ears of the heart' and come as we are and the Holy Spirit within us moves us to speak to Our Lady as to a friend.

The Joyful Mysteries are taken up with family life and with all the anxiety and happiness this entails. We turn to them, not seeking comfort in the familiarity of the earthly, but above all in acknowledgement of the unearthly and the extraordinary. We bring our life's experience not in order to find out how we may achieve success, but to see everything in proportion and in a clear light. We dwell on the scenes before us, we feel them and let our lives merge into them. From the confusion of everyday life, we step into a world whose values lead us to the essential and the eternal.

To those who are overwhelmed by loneliness and despair, the Sorrowful Mysteries have a particular significance. No one is immune to the suffering endemic in the world and each day brings fresh evidence of personal tragedy or disaster of mind-numbing proportion through the immediacy of the press. We struggle to understand these things in order to make our lives bearable. Such events sharpen our understanding of the agony in the garden, the betrayal of Jesus by his friends, the grief of those he loved and the dereliction of the cross. There can be few who have not experienced loneliness,

29

and the desolation of Christ on the cross is the expression of his love and assurance that when we are most alone, he is surely near us. For those who mourn, the image of Mary standing by her dying son can only bring the deepest consolation, and the closing words of the Hail Mary, quietly repeated, will bring great comfort.

The experience of God's presence has been compared to that rare and overwhelming sense of happiness which can occur when we are caught unawares, however momentary or unexpected the occurrence is that causes us to feel inexpressible happiness. This is often described as a fleeting knowledge of God, a brief and tantalizing awareness of that which he has prepared for us and which is beyond our wildest imaginings. The Glorious Mysteries spell out the manner in which this fleeting perception becomes reality. It can be deeply consoling to meditate upon the fact that those who were present and witnessed these events were no less bewildered.

Imperceptibly the emphasis shifts from our own existence and as we are absorbed into the meditation, the reality of the image gradually expands and fills the mind. Silence descends as the mind quietly moves forward into a different realm, subject only to the gentle reminder of the repeated *Aves*. The work of the Holy Spirit invades the heart and the mind, assisted by the prayer of Our Lady, for she 'kept these things in her heart' (Luke 2:19). Through her assistance we are brought to see and understand them.

The Joyful Mysteries

The First Joyful Mystery:
The Annunciation

In his engraving of the annunciation, David Jones
clearly shows the order of things, for the angel, who is
the messenger from heaven, bows in reverence before
Our Lady who in turn inclines her head in acknowledgement of this great honour. The angel Gabriel kneels
before the one who was chosen before time began (Genesis: 3:15) to be the mother of God. The angel is placed
on the earthly side of the picture and in the distance,
the garden echoes the garden of paradise and the tree
of knowledge. Mary is separated from this scene in an
atmosphere of prayer and calm. The angel carries a
lily, the sign of purity, as if to emphasize that the baby
will be of Adam, but not of the seed of Adam. It is an evo-
cation of heaven in obeisance and in tantalizing suspense, awaiting the acceptance of Mary.

Behind the angel, the gate that has been closed is open and the stream of grace flows through.

> *And in the sixth month the angel Gabriel was sent from God into a city of Galilee called Nazareth, to a Virgin espoused to a man whose name was Joseph, of the house of David; and the Virgin's name was Mary. And the angel, being come in, said unto her: Hail, full of grace, the Lord is with thee: blessed art thou among women. Who, having heard, was troubled at his saying and thought with herself what manner of salutation this should be. And the angel said to her: Fear not, Mary, for thou hast found grace with God. Behold, thou shalt conceive in thy womb and shalt bring forth a son; and thou shalt call his name Jesus. He shall be great and shall be called the Son of the Most High. And the Lord God shall give unto him the throne of David his father; and he shall reign in the house of Jacob forever. And of his kingdom there shall be no end. And Mary said to the angel: How shall this be, because I know not man? And the angel answering, said to her: The Holy Ghost shall come upon thee and the power of the Most High shall overshadow thee. And therefore also the holy one which shall be born of thee shall be called the Son of God. And, behold, thy cousin Elizabeth, she also hath conceived a son in her old age; and this is the sixth month with her that is called barren. Because no word shall be impossible with God. And Mary said: Behold the handmaid of the Lord; be it done to me according to thy word. And the angel departed from her.* (Luke 1:26–38)

Mary was a young girl of thirteen or fourteen when this event took place. As far as we know, she had been brought up by her parents, traditionally known as

St Anne and St Joachim, under the Jewish law. We know from the words of the angel that she was 'full of grace' and no more wonderful description could be given. For it tells us that she was a creature so pleasing to God that her soul was literally a reflection of divine love.

With her humility came also great prudence, for Our Lady was 'troubled at his saying and thought with herself what manner of salutation this should be'. She was calmed by the words of the angel, 'Fear not', and that in itself is astonishing. In the sheltered and peaceful tenor of her life, such a cosmic occurrence would be enough to unnerve the sturdiest heart, and the words of the angel which followed were no less alarming. For what followed was the announcement of the most important event in the history of the world since the banishment from paradise. The future of the human race hung in the balance for one tantalizing moment while heaven and earth were held in suspense awaiting Mary's *fiat* or acceptance.

Mary's trust in God prompted her to enquire of the angel the manner in which this event could take place, 'since I know not man'. One can only speculate on the consequences of the angel's request. Our Lady was betrothed to St Joseph but not yet married. At that time it was not unknown for a child to be born to a betrothed couple, and for such a child to be considered legitimate. If, however, the woman was found to have been unfaithful to her betrothed, death by stoning was the usual punishment. Joseph knew this to be unthinkable, but one can imagine the depth of his inward crisis.

Like all brought up in the Jewish faith, Mary's knowledge of the Scriptures was extensive and she must therefore have been somehow aware of the terrible suffering that awaited the Messiah, and of her own suffering which would be entailed in her acceptance.

None of these speculations appears to have clouded her submission and her acceptance of the will of God. And having received Our Lady's words, 'be it done to me according to thy word', the angel left her without any consoling explanation or comfort. But the future of the human race was assured.

The Second Joyful Mystery:
The Visitation

Elizabeth as the older woman is seated to receive the
greeting of her cousin, and in this way the artist emphasizes the homage of St John offered from his mother's
womb. John must look up to the child Our Lady carries.
Wherever she goes, Mary brings Jesus and as the haloes
of the two women merge, it is as if John the Baptist
greets his Lord. Zachariah is partly obscured and apart
from the scene. He is unable to accept the miracle
before him, and his feet are firmly placed in the everyday world. His head, inclined towards the holiness of
the room, hints at his dilemma.

*And Mary, rising up in those days went into the hill
country with haste into the city of Juda. And she*

> *entered into the house of Zachary and saluted Eliza-*
> *beth. And it came to pass that, when Elizabeth heard*
> *the salutation of Mary, the infant leaped in her*
> *womb; and Elizabeth was filled with the Holy Ghost.*
> *And she cried out with a loud voice and said: Blessed*
> *art thou among women and blessed is the fruit of thy*
> *womb. And whence is this to me that the mother of*
> *my Lord should come to me? For behold, as soon as*
> *the voice of thy salutation sounded in my ears, the*
> *infant in my womb leaped for joy. And blessed art*
> *thou that hast believed because these things shall be*
> *accomplished that were spoken to thee by the*
> *Lord.*   (Luke 1:39–45)

The journey Mary embarked upon was daunting. In a land that was rife with violence, she undertook the journey on foot, accompanied, according to tradition, by a single female attendant. Having accepted the will of God, Our Lady did not just sit back and await events. Knowing that her cousin was in need of her, she set off without hesitation to be with Elizabeth.

Our Lady brought the child within her to Elizabeth as she will bring him to us if we will turn to her. She need not have feared any lack of understanding on the part of Elizabeth. Inspired by the Holy Spirit, her cousin greets her with the words of the angel Gabriel, 'Blessed art thou amongst women ...' and the unborn John the Baptist leaps in greeting to his Lord.

The words of the Magnificat uttered by Mary in reply to Elizabeth remind us once more of the knowledge of the Old Testament which Mary possessed. Every line is full of allusion to the Bible in this joyful announcement that God had visited his people.

This is the longest utterance recorded of Our Lady, who is normally so sparing of words. It is interesting

that on this occasion Mary's humility takes a different
form and she is overwhelmed with joy.

> My soul doth magnify the Lord
> and my spirit hath rejoiced in God my
>   saviour,
> because he hath regarded the humility
>   of his handmaid;
> for behold from henceforth all
>   generations shall call me blessed
> because he that is mighty hath done
>   great things to me;
>   and holy is his name.
> And his mercy is from generation unto
>   generation,
>   to them that fear him.
> He hath shewed might in his arm; he
>   hath scattered the proud
>   in the conceit of their heart.
> He hath put down the mighty from
>   their seat and hath exalted the
>   humble.
> He hath filled the hungry with good
>   things; and the rich he hath sent
>   away empty.
> He hath received Israel his servant,
>   being mindful of his mercy
> as he spoke to our Fathers; to
>   Abraham and to his seed forever.
>   (Luke 1:46–55)

The Third Joyful Mystery:
The Nativity

Mary and Joseph gaze down in wonder and love at the child who lifts his arms in a gesture of giving, as if to foretell his death on the cross. The star glows above the shepherds who crowd in the entrance, and on the right the animals kneel. Above the scene of intimacy and love the Holy Spirit hovers in the form of a dove.

And it came to pass that when they were there her days were accomplished that she should be delivered. And she brought forth her first-born son and wrapped him in swaddling clothes and laid him in a manger because there was no room for them in the inn. And there were in the same country shepherds watching and keeping the night-watches over their flock. And behold, the angel of the Lord stood by them and the

41

> *brightness of God shone round about them; and they*
> *feared with a great fear. And the angel said to them:*
> *Fear not; for, behold, I bring you good tidings of*
> *great joy that shall be to all the people; For this day*
> *is born to you a saviour, who is Christ the Lord, in*
> *the city of David. And this shall be a sign unto you:*
> *You shall find the infant wrapped in swaddling*
> *clothes and laid in a manger. And suddenly there*
> *was with the angel a multitude of the heavenly army,*
> *praising God and saying: Glory to God in the highest;*
> *and on earth peace to men of good will.* (Luke 2:6–14)

Caesar Augustus was intent on his grandiose plan to take a census of the world. As far as the census-takers of the time were concerned, 'the world' meant the Roman Empire and notices went up everywhere ordering people to return to their town of origin in order to register. Despite the imminence of the birth of the holy child, Joseph felt impelled to set out immediately on the arduous journey from Nazareth to Bethlehem.

Joseph must have felt confident of finding shelter somewhere in his home town, despite the thronging crowd arriving from all directions in obedience to Caesar's command. As they went from door to door, becoming increasingly tired, it would have become apparent that Roman soldiers and other wealthy visitors had found shelter, but for them there was nothing. That sad line, 'There was no room at the inn', echoes forlornly in St Luke's Gospel. Eventually room – if it could be called that – was found in a stable beneath the inn, among the animals.

It is appropriate that the animals should be present at the birth of God made man. Untrammelled by human considerations, they stay quietly by the manger, unaware of the astounding event taking place in their midst, and resting peacefully in the presence of their maker.

Our Lord did not announce himself to the world. Through an angel his coming was made known to some shepherds, and the Wise Men were informed by a star. Two completely different sorts of people: the shepherds in their simplicity recognized divinity, and the Magi in their wisdom were not influenced by appearances.

The shepherds came immediately and did not find the poverty strange; they probably knew that King David had himself been a shepherd, and the words of the angel had filled them with joy. The Magi were slightly more cautious, as the clever have a tendency to be, and took the precaution of verifying the direction of the star at the court of King Herod – a fatal diversion.

To Herod the news was grim indeed. He feared the end of his reign with the coming of the Messianic King of the Jews and he sought to forestall the will of God by striking out violently against the innocent – the reaction of tyrants throughout history.

We wince in pity at the massacre of the innocents, which is repeated to this day in abortion clinics, in famine and in wars around the world. The birth of the holy child proclaims the sanctity of life and at the same time underlines the vulnerability of innocence that relies totally on the protective care and love of parents.

The old Roman word for charity, *caritas*, meant love of family or close relations; interested love rather than disinterested. After Bethlehem, charity was transformed by the love of the holy child into love for the entire human race. We see its fruits today when people separated by thousands of miles can be moved to loving pity and practical aid for others who are starving or suffering; in the work of Mother Teresa for the poor, and the work of hospices throughout the world where the

43

dying are cared for with love. Such disinterested love flows from the stable at Bethlehem.

Humility, too, has taken on a new meaning from the old understanding of lowness or meanness. Not the false modesty dictated by so-called good manners which obliges people to deny their God-given gifts, nor an obsequious fawning before superiors, but the humility of the man who silently and happily places others before himself, who accepts injustice without rancour. That is the humility that comes from Bethlehem where the Son of God was born in a stable.

The Fourth Joyful Mystery: The Presentation

Mary bends over her child with anxious tenderness as she presents him to Simeon, who in turn looks heavenwards as he kneels in the knowledge that this is the miracle he has awaited with such confidence. Anna stands holding the Scriptures foretelling the birth of a saviour while St Joseph, holding the two turtledoves, seems consumed with concern for Mary and her child.

And after the days of her purification, according to the law of Moses, were accomplished, they carried him to Jerusalem, to present him to the Lord. Every male opening the womb shall be called holy to the Lord; And to offer a sacrifice as it is written in the law of the Lord, a pair of turtledoves or two young pigeons.
Luke 2:22–24

Under the law of Moses, a mother was considered unclean after the birth of a child. So Mary had to present herself at the temple to be purified, at the same time presenting her first born son. Despite the fact that Mary was the mother of God, there was no exemption for her, neither in her humility did she ever seek to do other than follow the law in obedience.

Normally the offering was a lamb, but owing to their extreme poverty Our Lady and St Joseph were permitted to offer two turtledoves. We are told of that holy pair, Simeon and Anna, who were present in the temple. Simeon had waited and prayed throughout his long life in the temple and immediately recognized in the Holy Child, the Redeemer he had awaited for so many years. Inspired by the Holy Spirit he uttered the words of the Nunc Dimittis:

> Now thou dost dismiss thy servant, O
>   Lord, according to thy word in
>   peace;
> Because my eyes have seen thy
>   salvation
> Which thou hast prepared before the
>   face of all peoples;
> A light to the revelation of the
>   gentiles and the glory of thy people
>   Israel.   (Luke 2:29–32)

How patiently he had waited, and how wonderfully that patience was rewarded. Anna too had waited many lonely years for that same joy, and her patience was also rewarded. As for Our Lady, she was told that a sword of sorrow would pierce her heart, but she must have already feared this. We are protected from knowledge of the future, but for Our Lady her suffering was spelled out unmercifully while she held the baby in her arms.

The Fifth Joyful Mystery: The Finding in the Temple

Mary greets Jesus with joy and although he returns her embrace, his hands and the inclination of his body remain in a gesture of instruction to the row of solemn men of learning before him. We only see half the face of St Joseph, which is turned to Mary with concern. We see his pleasure at the reunion of Mary with her son, but apart from this he has little understanding of the scene before him.

And, when he was twelve years old, they were going up to Jerusalem, according to the custom of the feast, and having fulfilled the days, when they returned, the child Jesus remained in Jerusalem. And his parents knew it not. And thinking that he was in the company they came a day's journey and sought him

> *among their kinsfolk and acquaintances. And, not*
> *finding him, they returned to Jerusalem, seeking*
> *him. And it came to pass that, after three days, they*
> *found him in the temple, sitting in the midst of the doc-*
> *tors, hearing them and asking them questions. And*
> *all that heard him were astonished at his wisdom*
> *and his answers. And, seeing him, they wondered.*
> *And his mother said to him: Son, why hast thou done*
> *so to us? And he said to them: How is it that you sought*
> *me? Did you not know that I must be about my*
> *Father's business? And they understood not the word*
> *that he spoke unto them.* (Luke 2:42–50)

The holy family responds to the dictates of the law
which requires that all men should attend the three
great feasts of the Passover, Pentecost and Tabernacles.
On reaching the age of twelve, Jesus was considered
mature in the eyes of the law, and therefore was able to
join his parents for the first time.

The loss of Our Lord for three days is one of the seven
sorrows of Our Lady. Not only did she suffer as any
mother who loses a child, but in her heart she also
knew that her son would eventually be put to death by
his own people. Since Jesus had now reached maturity
she must have wondered if the time of his death was
upon them. Mary suffered the dark night of all who
lose God, and she was to suffer again for the three days
between the crucifixion and the resurrection.

In a sermon on the finding in the temple, the twelfth
century Abbot Aelred of Rievaulx pointed out that Our
Lord often withdraws himself for a short time, in order
to make us search more diligently for him. The mystery
of the finding in the temple therefore is the image of
the quest of the devout soul.

Apart from being relieved, Mary and Joseph must
have been amazed to find Jesus seated amongst the

pupils in the school of Rabbis before the learned priests and scribes: the child of twelve sitting calmly before the elders. Their minds are befuddled with layers of legislative knowledge and yet they listen attentively to the wisdom of their Lord and God. St Luke, with great economy of words, says simply that they were 'astonished'.

This mystery is firmly placed among the joys because of the contrast between the words of Jesus to his mother in the temple when he teaches us that the things of God must come before all that we love most in this world, and the image of life within the holy family evoked by St Luke at the end of this story.

> *And he went down with them and came to Nazareth and was subject to them. And his mother kept all these words in her heart. And Jesus advanced in wisdom and age and grace with God and men.*
>
> (Luke 2:52)

The Sorrowful Mysteries

The First Sorrowful Mystery:
The Agony in the Garden

Jesus kneels amongst the olive trees, arms outstretched in prayer, and his loneliness is accentuated by the sleeping disciples. Again the gate is portrayed, this time slightly ajar as redemption can only be completed by Jesus leaving the garden and enduring the suffering on the cross. From the direction of the city walls in the distance we can almost hear the rhythmic marching of the approaching mob whose faces are concealed by hoods, a strangely contemporary note. The river runs almost as a torrent as if to underline the impending violence, and the whole scene is bathed in eerie moonlight.

> *When Jesus had said these things, he went forth with his disciples over the brook Cedron where there was a garden, into which he entered with his disciples.*
> (John 18:1)

As if to underline the rocky nature of the countryside, St Luke describes Our Lord withdrawing from the others a 'stone's cast'. The rocks must have cast foreboding shadows across the hill, the twisted limbs of the olive trees standing eerily on the skyline like some distended cross, announcing the gathering forces of evil to an already bleak scene. The sounds of the gathering mob in the distance, the shouts and the cracking of sticks being torn from the ground, all carried on the still night air to the place where Jesus knelt.

Even in his hour of desolation, Jesus still teaches us with loving awareness of our weakness. To what immense lengths we will go to avoid suffering; whole industries are involved in producing panaceas for every ill. Any suffering is believed to be a grievous injustice: it is the 'right' of every person to be free from all discomfort. To the saints, suffering became the very means of salvation. Our Lord prayed until his sweat turned to drops of blood, for through his divinity Christ knew precisely what was to befall him during the hours of excruciating torture that lay ahead, and even more serious was the knowledge of the sin that would continue to be committed and unrepented until the end of time. He prayed, 'My Father, if this chalice may not pass away but I must drink it, thy will be done' (Matthew 26:42).

We are told of the angel who was sent to comfort Our Lord and there is another aspect to be pondered over in this desolate scene. Our Lord had turned for comfort to the three disciples: Peter, the rock on which he would found his Church; John, the beloved and his brother, James – and they responded by falling asleep. The New Testament has several warnings to us to remain spiritually alert; and above all the words of Jesus to the three disciples: 'Watch ye; and pray that you enter not into temptation. The spirit indeed is will-

ing, but the flesh is weak' (Mark 14:38). Eventually their
drowsy watch is brought to an abrupt halt as the din of
the approaching mob grows louder, and they go forward
to meet the crowd.

The Second Sorrowful Mystery:
The Scourging at the Pillar

Jesus is tied to the pillar, his arms extended above his head in order that the pain inflicted may be the more severe. Two soldiers are chosen to inflict the stripes, their muscles extended by their exertions. The curiosity and fascination of the soldiers witnessing the scene is without pity.

They therefore being gathered together, Pilate said: Whom will you that I release to you, Barabbas, or Jesus that is called Christ? For he knew that for envy they had delivered him. And as he was sitting in the place of judgment, his wife sent to him, saying: Have thou nothing to do with that just man; for I have suffered many things this day in a dream because of him. But the chief priests and ancients persuaded the

> *people, that they should ask Barabbas, and make*
> *Jesus away. And the governor answering, said to*
> *them: Whether will you of the two to be released unto*
> *you? But they said Barabbas. Pilate saith to them:*
> *What shall I do then with Jesus that is called Christ?*
> *They say all: Let him be crucified.*
>
> (Matthew 27: 17–22)

And along they all come, egging each other on with shouts and waving arms until anti-climactically they come to a clattering halt in front of Jesus. Lost for the moment, they seem unable to decide on their next move, standing there rather stupidly; and St John tells us that Judas stood with them. And when Jesus quietly enquires of this sea of faces, 'Whom seek ye?' and replies to their demand, 'I am he', they stumble backwards, falling over each other.

For one precious second, the voice of innocence silences evil, but the betrayal of Judas ensures that the crowd, now even more enraged by shame, grab Jesus and to justify their fury, bind his hands with rope. Such is the power of innocence that this huge mob felt safe only when Our Lord, alone and defenceless, was tightly bound. For now we know the blunt truth, which is that the disciples had abandoned Jesus and run away into the night. St John tells us that Jesus was first led to Annas, before being taken on to his son-in-law, Caiaphas, the high priest. And there, the priests, elders and scribes looked for some means of condemning Jesus.

There was no shortage of people rushing forward to invent accusations, but even in these extraordinary circumstances, the evidence was ludicrous. Eventually the high priest rose to his feet, subduing the rabble to ask Jesus if he was indeed 'the Christ, the son of God', to which he replied, 'Thou hast said it.' Triumphant that he might at last have a case the high priest, like any tyrant, turns to his cowed followers for approval. But another problem now looms for the mob: their law forbade them to put a man to death, they could go no further than the reply that Jesus was 'guilty of death'. Someone else must be found to carry out that sentence, and they knew that Pontius Pilate was their man.

Pilate is mystified at first by the babbling of vague accusations, 'We have found this man perverting our nation, and forbidding us to give tribute to Caesar'. In St John's account, the chief priests appear even more uneasy, unable to find anything more convincing than 'if he were not a malefactor, we would not have delivered him up to you'. But Pilate grasps the reason for their envy and hatred: they are saying that Jesus has proclaimed himself their King. Pilate now understands the situation, as far as he is able, and knows what the Jewish leaders require of him. He is in an agony of indecision. When he hears the words of Jesus, 'Everyone that is of the truth heareth my word', he replies wearily, 'What is truth?', and he returns to the crowd saying, 'I find no cause in him'. He offers to release one prisoner to them as was the custom on the Feast of Passover. They take up his offer and choose Barabbas and, amid shouts of 'crucify him' when he suggests Jesus be released instead, Pilate capitulates to the rule of the mob. How blind we are in our efforts to save our skin in the eyes of the world; but Pilate has one last, desperate card to play. In sending Our Lord to be scourged, he clung to the hope that the bloodlust of Jesus' enemies might thus be satisfied and they would be shamed into releasing him. This was the greatest cruelty. Scourging was often inflicted on the condemned man before crucifixion. It was inflicted by several soldiers with metal-tipped leather thongs and continued until a state of excruciating physical agony was achieved, but it stopped short of death in order to ensure that the victim could still suffer on the cross.

The Third Sorrowful Mystery:
The Crowning with Thorns

The soldiers now crowd around Jesus, in their effort to mock and ridicule the figure before them. They even make crude obeisance before him, laughing at his pain. He sits in dignity, his head bowed in compassion and forgiveness and his hand raised in blessing, for 'they know not what they do'.

> *And they clothed him with purple; and, platting a crown of thorns, they put it upon him. And they began to salute him; Hail, king of the Jews. And they struck his head with a reed; and they did spit on him. And bowing their knees, they adored him.*
>
> (Mark 15:17–19)

Here, if ever it was needed, is the evidence that things

are rarely as they appear. This sad and bleeding figure is the saviour of the world. Earthly kings and leaders are usually surrounded by pomp and circumstance, and today, with layers of security, and yet this pathetic figure was the Son of God, the King of all kings, the Creator of the world that now mocks him and spits upon him. The sin of mankind gives vent to terrible vengeance and Jesus freely accepts torture and death for our sin. His love for his creation is beyond all human comprehension.

The irony of the situation is intentional. One of the principal reasons for the hatred of the chief priests was Our Lord's claim to be the King of the Jews. They were well aware that a final, messianic age had been foretold in the prophecies of the Old Testament, and now, these prophecies were being strongly and painfully fulfilled. For the soldiers, who had so cruelly beaten the prisoner, no biblical predictions clouded their minds. They merely looked upon such claimants, to kingship and divinity – and there were several – as tiresome troublemakers causing civil disturbance and putting more work on the military.

And now, with all the energy of bullies let loose upon the innocent, the soldiers set about Jesus, crushing a circlet of thorns into his forehead. Seeing the blood pouring down his face onto the cloak which was already clinging to his open wounds, their sarcasm knows no bounds. They kneel before Jesus, sneering in mock obeisance. Having handed him the 'sceptre' of weakness, a reed, they snatch it from him and start to drive the thorns more deeply into his brow as they strike his head and face.

And then it appears that Pilate, the man, separates himself from Pilate the Governor, and is alone before his Creator. With almost childlike curiosity Pilate asks Jesus where he comes from. He is made even more uneasy by Jesus' silence, and reminds him that he, Pilate, has the power to crucify him or set him free. Our Lord replies, 'Thou shouldst not have any power against me, unless it were given thee from above. Therefore he that hath delivered me to thee hath the greater sin' (John 19:11). In that moment of truth, with the eyes of Our Lord upon him, Pilate seeks to escape the dreadful predicament in which he finds himself. But the roar of the crowd overwhelms him, and the punishment that Caesar would inflict on him for misrule seems more real than the injustice he is about to mete out on Christ. Pilate succumbs.

In one final futile jibe at the crowd, Pilate asks them if he should crucify their king. In a deafening shout, the chief priests reject the kingship of Christ and Jesus is led away.

The Fourth Sorrowful Mystery:
The Carrying of the Cross

Jesus bows down beneath the weight of the cross, the soldiers wielding sticks goad him and one is even leaning on the cross to increase its already dreadful weight. The grieving women, their hands joined in prayer, lean tenderly towards him as he passes by.

> *Then therefore he delivered him to them to be crucified. And they took Jesus and led him forth. And bearing his own cross, he went forth to that place which is called Calvary, but in Hebrew Golgotha.*
>
> (John 19:16–17)

Within the space of one week, something had changed the peaceful, rejoicing crowd of Palm Sunday, with their joyful chant of 'Hosannah' into the vengeful mob with its roar of 'Crucify him'.

To all intents and purposes, this was a democratic choice; the choice of the people to bludgeon vacillating authority at the cost of the innocent. Propaganda and public opinion (which often means nothing of the sort) had been at work. The chief priests and their followers, aware that their grip of events was threatened, moved into action. Their emissaries may well have gone from house to house spreading deceit and inciting hatred.

Some of those who had hailed Jesus only a week before, were perhaps among those who now disowned him as he was led beyond the city walls to the place of crucifixion.

The procession is made up of officials, the centurion with his detachment of soldiers, the two thieves and Our Lord. They make their way through the crowd, silent at last, apart from the few jeers still to be heard from stragglers hurrying to catch up, fearful of missing a moment of the drama.

The cross was roughly thrust onto the torn and bleeding shoulders of Christ. Splinters would have pressed into his shoulder as he moved forward under its great weight. Isaiah had foretold that 'his government would be on his shoulder' (Isaiah 9:5) and Our Lord himself had said, 'And he that taketh not up his cross and followeth me, is not worthy of me' (Matthew 10:38). And again, 'If any man will come after me, let him deny himself, and take up his cross and follow me. For he that will save his life will lose it; and he that shall lose his life for my sake shall find it' (Matthew 16:24). The way of the cross demonstrates to us that the path to heaven is made up of one small step at a time in patience and self-denial, following the road to Calvary.

The soldiers were fearful that if Jesus fell yet again under the weight of the cross he might die before reaching Calvary. They looked around for someone to carry the cross, because this task was too demeaning for a Roman soldier. Their eyes fell on a visitor amongst the crowd, one Simon of Cyrene, unknown until now, but to be remembered for all time for this one brief moment. Simon was probably unwilling to be pulled into the drama but rose to the occasion and took up his burden. Some who have suffering thrust upon them accept it with resignation and even joy, as the means of salvation. Simon of Cyrene must have been such a one, for St Mark's Gospel implies that his sons, Alexander and Rufus, no doubt influenced by the action of their father, became Christians (Mark 15:21).

Simon was not the only one in that hostile crowd to be moved with pity for Our Lord, although most of his disciples and friends seem to have vanished with undignified haste. Women do not appear to have been amongst those who called for his blood: 'His blood be upon us and upon our children' (Matthew 27:25). The only woman who makes an appearance during the trial is the wife of Pilate who so urgently begged him to have nothing to do with Our Lord (Matthew 27:19). Legend describes Veronica bravely making her way through the crowd to wipe the dirt and blood from the face of Jesus with a linen cloth. Her love must have been brave and certain to enable her to elbow her way through that angry mob, probably pushing and shoving her, and jeering at her courage.

And the women of Jerusalem weep in pity. Jesus stops and breaks his silence. At a time when he might have been overwhelmed with grief and suffering, he speaks words of comfort and concern for them. 'Daughters of Jerusalem, weep not over me; but weep for yourselves and for your children. For, behold, the day shall come, wherein they will say; Blessed are the barren and the wombs that have not borne and the paps that have not given suck. Then shall they begin to say to the mountains; fall upon us, and to the hills; cover us. For if in the green wood they do these things, what shall be done in the dry?' (Luke 23:28–31).

He was the 'green wood', the tree of life; the 'dry wood' was the doomed city of Jerusalem, and later the world which would be deaf to his word. Having spoken these words, he went on his way until the hill of Calvary was reached.

The Fifth Sorrowful mystery:
The Crucifixion

'Sweet Christ's dear Tree!' are David Jones' own words.

Jesus hangs on the cross. His mother Mary and St John stand beneath him, mute in their grief, while Mary Magdalene embraces his dying body. Jesus turns to the good thief who turns his face trustingly towards him, while the bad thief hangs his head in bitterness. The motionless figure of the centurion is strangely moving, for we know that he watches the scene with a growing awareness of the significance of the figure before him.

> *And it was almost the sixth hour: and there was darkness over all the earth until the ninth hour. And the sun was darkened and the veil of the temple was rent in the midst. And Jesus, crying with a loud voice,*

> *said: Father, into thy hands I commend my spirit.*
> *And saying this he gave up the ghost. Now, the centur-*
> *ion seeing what was done, glorified God, saying:*
> *'Indeed this was a just man.'*   (Luke 23:44–47)

Death ultimately means the punishment of sin. Until the sin of Adam, death had no place in God's plan. Until the sting of death was drawn by Jesus there was no hope for mankind. As Jesus arrived at Calvary, the gruesome act of sacrifice entered its final stage.

Having roughly torn the clothes from the body of Christ, the soldiers prepare to nail his hands and feet to the arms and upright beam of the cross. The precise positioning of the nails was a carefully calculated means of inflicting the greatest pain, while at the same time ensuring that the hands were not actually torn from the wrists. Their fearful work done, the last hammer blow echoes around the city walls below, the cross is lifted and placed in the pit prepared for it. The extended, pinioned arms of Jesus take his full weight as he hangs before the soldiers, who are now exhausted by their task.

Those who were crucified would sometimes, in their excruciating pain, shout down foul abuse on those who passed by. In his agony, Our Lord's concern was for his persecutors: 'Father forgive them for they know not what they do.' Any human tragedy will always attract the curious and while this scene unfolds, the people remain, staring in fascination. 'And they stood and watched him,' says St Matthew; the other evangelists making the same calm yet reproachful observation.

Egged on by the rapt attention of the crowd, the chief priests and onlookers taunt Jesus, urging him to prove he is Israel's king and God's Son by coming down from the cross and saving himself (Matthew 27:39–44). Jesus could certainly have accepted their challenge and come down from the cross, fully restored to healthy manhood. But all that took place had in fact been foretold: Jesus came down to earth in order to take mankind to paradise. His sacrifice for the salvation of man had been anticipated from the time of the fall. In the bleak garden of Calvary, redemption was achieved.

On either side of Jesus were crucified the two thieves. The first one, like many criminals before and after, cursed his fate and swore at the onlookers although his punishment, horrific as it was, was in accordance with the law of the time. The second thief understood this but said to Jesus, 'Lord, remember me when thou shalt come into thy Kingdom. And Jesus said to him: Amen, I say to thee; This day thou shalt be with me in paradise' (Luke 23:42–43). How strange to think that the first person to follow Our Lord into paradise was a condemned thief who was the first to receive the fruits of Calvary. The centurion who had supervised the crucifixion also made his confession of faith at Calvary and would enter paradise.

After three hours of agony Our Lord was close to death. Silhouetted against a darkening sky were the figures of John the beloved disciple and Mary, his mother, standing bowed in grief at the foot of the cross. What must have been their thoughts? The other disciples had fled and were hiding in the shadows of the city. Only St John, Our Lady and some other women remained. They cannot have fully understood what was happening. They saw only that their beloved was hanging, bleeding and dying, before them. Mary had known from the beginning that a sword would pierce her heart, but no warning could have prepared her for this. In the gathering gloom, they heard the voice of Jesus coming down to them deep and true, unbroken by pain. 'When Jesus therefore had seen his mother and the disciple standing, whom he loved, he saith to his mother: Woman, behold thy son' (John 19:26). By addressing his mother as 'Woman' Jesus was reminding us of the words of Genesis 3:15, 'And I will put enmity between thee and the woman, and between thy seed, and her seed; it shall bruise thy head, and thou shalt bruise his heel' (A.V.). She was that woman, and he was her seed. Only through her *fiat*, or acceptance of the angel's message was God's plan carried out. She was there too at the final act of redemption.

How can we ignore his dying request to St John that his grieving mother should be honoured? And Jesus made us the astonishing gift of Mary as our heavenly mother, in his words to St John, 'Son, behold thy mother'. Who could carry our imperfect prayers more perfectly to her Son, than Mary? The prayer of the rosary brings us close to Calvary, to stand silently by those two figures at the foot of the cross.

'And bowing his head, he gave up the ghost' (John 19:30).

The Glorious Mysteries

The First Glorious Mystery:
The Resurrection

The stone is rolled away from the dark and cavernous tomb, the stream of grace is flowing from it. In the midst of a garden of flowers and olive trees Jesus is risen again. His head is inclined in gentle reassurance to Mary Magdalene; his hands, marked by the nails, are raised in blessing. Mary kneels, her face raised in happiness as she greets her Lord.

And when the Sabbath was past, Mary Magdalene and Mary the mother of James and Salome bought sweet spices, that coming they might anoint Jesus. And very early in the morning, the first day of the week, they came to the sepulchre, the sun being now risen. And they said to one another; Who shall roll back the stone from the door of the sepulchre? And,

> *looking into the sepulchre, they saw a young man sit-*
> *ting on the right side, clothed with a white robe; and*
> *they were astonished. Who said to them: be not frigh-*
> *tened. You seek Jesus of Nazareth, who was crucified.*
> *He is risen; he is not here. Behold the place where*
> *they laid him. But go, tell his disciples, and Peter*
> *that he goeth before you into Galilee. Therefore you*
> *shall see him, as he told you.* (Mark 16:1–7)

The secret friends of Jesus, those who had visited him at night, now take their honoured place in history. Joseph of Arimathea had been to see Pilate to ask for the body of Christ, and, together with Nicodemus and a few devoted followers, they prepared to take Our Lord down from the cross. Mary must have been present, as they carefully lifted the torn limbs from the grip of the nails and removed the thorns from his brow, before they placed him in her arms. How different were the thoughts of the woman who now, in anguish, held the broken body of her son from the feelings of the young mother who had smiled down on her child so many years before. They anointed the body with myrrh and spices and wrapped it carefully in white linen. St John says, 'Now there was in the place where he was crucified a garden; and in the garden a new sepulchre, wherein no man yet had been laid' (John 19:41). And there they laid him, rolling a large stone across the entrance before vanishing into the night and into obscurity.

What can have been the thoughts of the disciples? They had fled from the scene before the trial of Our Lord and nothing had been heard of them since. They were cowering in fear, heartbroken at the turn of events and, in their panic, completely forgetting that on many occasions they had been warned of what lay ahead. How often we doubt the promises of Christ. Apart from anything else, we feel that we are not up to much and certainly do not merit the future he holds out to us, so we turn away. While no one can ever 'deserve' redemption, we reject salvation if we fail to take literally the words of Christ. He had told the disciples that he would rise again on the third day, but none of them believed it.

Ironically it appears that the only ones to place any faith in his words were the chief priests and the pharisees, and they hurriedly dispatched soldiers to mount guard on the tomb (Matthew 27:62–64). They even set a time limit of three days on the guard, revealing their fear of the words of Christ, 'I will destroy this temple made with hands, and within three days I will build another not made with hands' (Mark 14:58). In some confused way they believed that only the theft of the body by the disciples could enable this promise to be fulfilled.

At dawn on the morning after the Sabbath, Mary Magdalene, Mary the mother of James, and Salome came to the tomb to embalm the body and to seek consolation in their grief. To their astonishment the stone was now rolled away and an angel was seated inside the tomb and was saying 'Fear not', just as the angel had said at the Annunciation. The angel told them the astounding news that Jesus was risen, and was on his way to Galilee, and, with that wonderful concern of heaven for the faint, but loving, hearted he added, 'Go quickly, tell his disciples that he is risen.'

And still the disciples cannot believe it. 'And these words seemed to them as idle tales; and they did not believe them' (Luke 24:11); while later, two other disciples of Jesus walk to Emmaus and are so preoccupied with their grief that they fail to recognize the figure who falls into step beside them. In reply to his gentle questioning, they become voluble and chatter on about the depth of their misery, incapable of hearing or understanding the long list of prophecies foretelling all that had taken place and with which the stranger rebukes them. It is only when Our Lord breaks bread with them that we are told: 'And their eyes were opened; and they knew him.' St Thomas, one of the twelve, even needed to plunge his fingers into the wounded hands before he could accept the risen Christ.

It is perhaps a small consolation to our wavering faith that even those who knew Jesus failed to believe him. But if they had believed more readily perhaps we would have found it more difficult. 'Their infirmity', says St Gregory, 'was, if I may so put it, our future firmness.'

The whole argument of faith rests on this mystery of the resurrection. St Paul says that if it is not a fact that Christ rose from the dead, then our faith is in vain (I Corinthians 15:14). The feast of Easter is the greatest feast of the Church's year and as the Easter candle springs into life, we celebrate a rebirth and promise of resurrection for each and every one in his creation.

For 'he rose again, according to the scriptures' (I Corinthians 15:4).

The Second Glorious Mystery:
The Ascension

With Mary in their midst, the eleven apostles watch with uplifted faces as Jesus goes up into heaven. In his hand, Peter holds the keys to the kingdom of heaven.

> *And it came to pass, whilst he blessed them, he departed from them and was carried up to heaven.*
> (Luke 24:51)

The mystery of the ascension always seems to carry an air of sadness. The disciples had only just begun to understand the reality of the resurrection, and their joy at the presence of Jesus in their midst must have been overwhelming. And yet he was to leave them once more. Again, they had been warned, and were at least consistent in once more failing to understand the words Our Lord spoke to them. They were happy to be with him and how achingly sad they must have felt when before their eyes, 'whilst he blessed them, he departed from them and was carried up to heaven' (Luke 24:51). When Luke tells the story of the ascension again in the Book of Acts, he describes the disciples gaping in such astonishment that the angels say, 'Ye men of Galilee, why stand you looking up to heaven? this Jesus who is taken up from you into heaven shall so come as you have seen him going to heaven' (Acts 1:9–11). And then they must have come to their senses, for the Gospel of Luke continues, 'And they adoring, went back to Jerusalem with great joy' (24:52). Why should they be so full of joy on this occasion when only forty days before they had run for cover when Our Lord was taken from them for the first time? Something tremendous had happened in those forty days. His resurrection had transformed their lives.

'Go and tell Peter,' the angel at the sepulchre had told the three women (Mark 16:7). Peter, who some three days earlier had denied any knowledge of Jesus; Peter, who ran all the way to the sepulchre (John 20:3–10) unable to believe or understand the words of Mary Magdalene, hardly daring to hope as he stared at the empty shroud – dear, marvellous, impetuous St Peter who was so astonished to see Our Lord when he appeared by the lake at Galilee that he promptly jumped out of the boat in his joy. And when he had finally recovered himself and Our Lord asked him if he loved him, St Peter was mystified that he should even ask. His love was unwavering when Jesus had asked him who people said he was. On that occasion Our Lord had said, 'Thou art Peter and upon this rock I shall build my Church. And the gates of hell shall not prevail against it.' St Peter seems to have made a muddle of most things after that – trying to dissuade Jesus from the cross, because he loved him, falling asleep when Our Lord asked him to watch with him in the garden of olives and denying him three times on the night of his trial. And yet the angel was quite specific that it was Peter who was to be told that Jesus had risen.

The risen Lord had first appeared to a woman who had had seven demons driven from her (Luke 8:2), and then to Peter who had denied him – both of them sinners who had repented. We have only to think of that look Our Lord gave St Peter after his third denial to realize how bitterly St Peter had wept. Upon that rock the Church was indeed founded and Peter was to die the same death as his Lord, only legend has it that he insisted he was unworthy of such honour, and was crucified upside down.

> *And Jesus, coming, spoke to them saying: all power is given to me in heaven and in earth. Go, therefore teach ye all nations; baptising them in the name of the Father and of the Son and of the Holy Spirit, teaching them to observe all things whatsoever I have commanded you. And, behold, I am with you all days, even to the consummation of the world.*
>
> (Matthew 28:18–20)

The Third Glorious Mystery:
The Descent of the Holy Spirit

The apostles are gathered in the upper room with Mary in their midst. The Holy Spirit descends with shafts of light. Gone is the paradise garden to be replaced by the world in which the apostles will spread the word.

And when the days of the Pentecost were accomplished they were all together in one place. And suddenly there came a sound from heaven, as of a mighty wind coming; and it filled the whole house where they were sitting. And there appeared to them parted tongues, as it were of fire; and it sat upon every one of them. And they were filled with the Holy Ghost; and they began to speak with divers tongues, according as the Holy Ghost would have them to speak.

(Acts 2:1–4)

From the moment of the resurrection, Jesus was preparing the disciples for the work that lay ahead, first calming their fears and their disbelief and then teaching them as their awakening understanding transformed them beyond recognition. 'Then he opened their understanding, that they might understand the scriptures' (Luke 24:45).

The city of Jerusalem was thronging with crowds drawn by the harvest festival when the disciples, with Mary and the holy women, gathered together in prayer to await the promised coming of the Holy Spirit.

The effect of Pentecost must have been astonishing. A wind suddenly arose around the building, and the crowds gathered in Jerusalem came running from all directions to see light in the form of flames hovering over the heads of the disciples. Even more astonishing was the ease with which the disciples then spoke to each and every person in his own language, for the crowds had come from many different areas. At first the crowd accused them of being drunk, but Peter rose to rebuke them. There was no uncertainty about him now and there was no hesitation as he spoke. When the crowd had heard him out, those same men who had sneered at the disciples only minutes before, became the first fruits of the Holy Spirit. 'What shall we do?' they asked Peter and he preached penance to them and baptized, we are told, about three thousand souls.

Through his special gifts the Holy Spirit inspires and guides the Church and all its members, if we will allow him to do so. No one person can change the will of another; we may be influenced and cajoled but never forcibly changed. The millions spent on the so-called hidden persuasion of advertising, and the mysterious workings of the psychiatric wards, are a measure of the effort required to attempt the impossible. God alone can change our wills through the workings of the Holy

Spirit, who abides in the soul from the moment of baptism, unless we forcibly eject him through sin. Sometimes it seems that we achieve only one small step at a time, before darkness engulfs us. But the gifts of the Holy Spirit are always there for the asking, and give us a true sense of proportion.

The Fourth Glorious Mystery:
The Assumption of Our Lady

Mary seems already to be part of another world as she gazes towards heaven, her hands raised in prayer. The lilies by her side denote her purity, the star echoing the star of Bethlehem. The angels burn incense in her honour.

Very little if anything is known of the years that remained to Our Lady after the death and resurrection of her Son. We know that she was with the disciples at Pentecost, and one tradition has it that she lived until the age of sixty-three. She is very likely to have lived peacefully amongst the disciples and we can be certain that she prayed for the young Church.

We are left in complete ignorance of any words she may have spoken, for her words were recorded on only four occasions. The last reported words spoken by

Mary were uttered at the marriage feast at Cana, when, having responded to the need of the hosts by speaking to her Son, Our Lady said to the servants: 'Whatsoever he shall say to you, do ye' (John 2:5). Throughout the entire New Testament, this is the only command Mary gives. Her eternal role as intercessor is underlined by her love for her Son and her loving concern for his creatures and the knowledge that only by doing his will can we be truly content. This single command tells us everything we need to know.

As a human being, Our Lady was bound by the laws of nature, and death is part of that law. As the one creature born without original sin, there was nothing to keep her in the grave; Satan held no sway whatsoever over this immaculate person.

Nowadays, 'tradition' sometimes has a quaintly folksy image, but within the Church tradition refers to the teaching handed down from the apostles, from one generation to the next, in an unceasing chain. The traditional teaching of the assumption of Mary had been accepted from time immemorial in both east and west and was a subject of meditation in the Glorious Mysteries of the rosary from the thirteenth century, long before the final seal of papal approval in the declaration of the Doctrine of the Assumption in 1950.

The assumption is the great promise to mankind. Our Lady had to die, but she was assumed body and soul into heaven as we shall be. For her there was no shadow of death, as her sinless state freed her from the grave. We must await the final day, but, forgiven through the sacrifice of Christ, we have the evidence of the assumption to fill us with optimism and hope.

The Fifth Glorious Mystery: The Crowning of Our Lady and the Glory of all the Saints

In this final engraving, Our Lord gently and tenderly places the crown on his mother's bowed head. It is an image of inexpressible love. The only people to witness this intimate scene are the saints. How wonderful must have been that meeting between the Son and his mother. The Son who had been born in a stable, and had lived subject to her, and the mother who had never protested during the agonizing betrayal and the death that had taken place before her stricken eyes.

This decade is devoted to the meeting between God and the one creature who so perfectly responded to his grace that she became the new Eve: the perfection of his creation who would restore all that had been lost in the Garden of Eden when the human race began its

89

long straggling march to Calvary. Perfection is almost impossible for most of us to imagine. So far is it from our comprehension, that we have manoeuvred the meaning to something more bearable and material, trivializing its real meaning. In the same way the word 'divine' has been casually misplaced without understanding.

The angel Gabriel told us at the annunciation that Mary was full of grace, and so completely in favour with God, that perhaps she was the only contemplative who never needed to place any 'obstacle' between herself and the world in order to speak with God. How often we think that all we need is to find some peaceful oasis in order to escape the muddles that surround us and open our hearts to God.

The personality of Our Lady was so full of humility that she is never mentioned for herself, but only in relation to the actions of her Son. As the mother of God, she is the most important woman there has ever been or ever will be. Paintings on the walls of the catacombs show her carrying the child Jesus, and the early Christians gradually became aware of her significance and realized that her own glory was necessary in order to magnify the glory of her Son. Devotion to Mary increased and at the General Council held at Ephesus in 431, the term 'Mother of God' (*Theotokos*) was decreed. Our Lady herself was all silence and humility; her glory lay in her relationship to her Son.

Our Lady is closer to God than all the hosts of angels and saints, and yet she is the most holy mother of all humanity to whom she has given her crown of the rosary. The future is in our hands, and how little we have to fear if within those hands are held the beads of the rosary.